IMAGES
of America

MONTGOMERY
CAPITAL CITY CORNERS

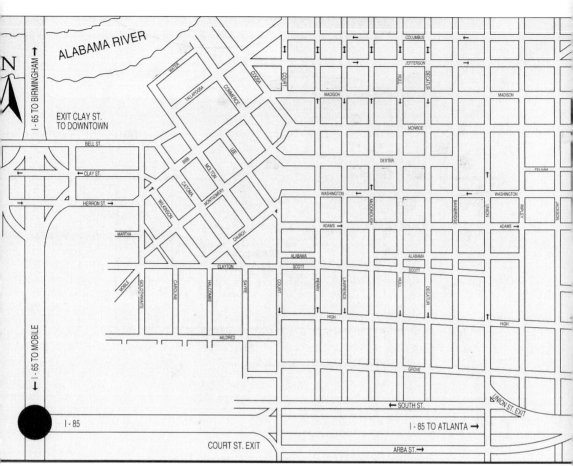

Montgomery's Center City.

IMAGES
of America

MONTGOMERY
CAPITAL CITY CORNERS

Mary Ann Neeley

ARCADIA

First published 1997
Copyright © Mary Ann Neeley, 1997

ISBN 0-7524-0553-5

Published by Arcadia Publishing,
an imprint of the Chalford Publishing Corporation,
One Washington Center, Dover, New Hampshire 03820.
Printed in Great Britain

Library of Congress Cataloging-in-Publication Data applied for

To my grandchildren,
Anna Young, Carrie, Collier, Graham and Mary Ellen Neeley,
I dedicate this book in hopes that they, too,
will find joy and satisfaction in discovering the past.

Contents

Acknowledgments

No work is ever accomplished without a great deal of support and assistance from those around who, if nothing else, have to tolerate neglect, benign or otherwise. In this case, my grateful appreciation goes out to family, friends, and fellow workers who have demonstrated patience far beyond what I will ever deserve. My husband, who gave up eating as his contribution to the project, receives special commendations and promises of at least one meal a week from this date forward.

Then, there are those who contributed untold hours to reading and re-reading the text, advising, correcting, and offering continuing encouragement. Edith Crook never faltered in this capacity, and Alta Cassady was always on hand to assist.

Pictures from many photographic collections, public and private, comprise this book; the largest represented is that of the Alabama Department of Archives and History (cited as ADAH). Robert Fouts of Fouts Photographic Services has an outstanding collection of historic negatives, many collected by John and June Scott. Working with an author who didn't always know exactly what she wanted, Robert exhibited admirable forbearance, copying photographs up to the last possible minute. The photographs were the works of amateur and professional photographers who recorded what they perceived significant to their world and the lives they lived. These included, among others, Bama Milner, Stanley Paulger, Franklin Collier, David Savlar, and Joe Holloway Jr. Ken Reynolds spent Sundays out on deserted streets capturing current scenes. We are indebted to all of these and countless others, many nameless, who have shared their times with ours through photographs. In addition to my thanks to these, I want to express my gratitude to a good friend and former co-author, Beth Taylor Muskat, who taught me to better understand old photographs and the information to be derived from them. The work we did together on the book *The Way It Was* prepared me, in some small way, for this publication. And while many were generous with time and assistance, only I bear the responsibility for any errors of omission or commission contained within the covers of this book.

PHOTOGRAPHIC COLLECTIONS REPRESENTED IN THIS BOOK:

Alabama Department of Archives and History; Landmarks Foundation of Montgomery, Inc.; Algernon Blair; *1894 Art Works of Montgomery*; *1907 Art Works of Montgomery*; Franklin and Betty Collier; Ken Reynolds; John and June Scott; Philadelphia Museum of Art; Mike McEachern; Frank and Betty Roton; Library of Congress; Mary Collier Oglesby; Dexter Avenue Methodist Church; David Savlar; Joe Holloway Jr.; Maurer and Julia Maurer; Alabama Bureau of Tourism and Travel; Hobbie family; Carole Turner; Fouts Photographic Services; Fred Drehr; Air University Library, Maxwell AFB; Davidson/Freeborn; Lanny and Julie Crane; Marilyn Sullivan; Alma Mareno McClurkin; Henry Hattemer; Charles M. Crook; Birmingham Public Library; University Library and Resource Center, Alabama State University; Mrs. W. Gordon Range; Walter and Allen James; David Gorrie; Robert Arrington; Frances Trott; Dr. and Mrs. Julius Pryor; Rebecca Starr; Kathryn Tucker Windham; Mary Louise Pugh; Betty McDuffee; and the Old South Historical Society.

Introduction

Montgomery, Alabama, a riverport town in the midst of cotton country, is a child of the War of 1812 and the Industrial Revolution. The former destroyed the power of the Creeks, Native Americans who once called Central Alabama home, and the latter brought cotton textiles to the attention of the world.

The Creeks once presided over much of Alabama and southwest Georgia, but in 1814 they suffered a disastrous defeat at Horseshoe Bend, at the hands of Andrew Jackson and his Tennessee Volunteers. The vanquished Creeks ceded millions of acres west of the Coosa to the United States. Eager Americans anticipated acquiring cheap, fertile land, growing cotton, and making money in the newly opened territory. Others saw the possibility of succeeding by providing the many services needed to support farmers and planters on the raw frontier.

The development of mechanical spinning and weaving devices in the mid-eighteenth century created a demand for cotton as the world began to appreciate its versatility. By the early nineteenth century, the Industrial Revolution was in full swing, with the manufacturing of cotton textiles playing a major role in its success. Along the seacoast of Georgia and South Carolina and on the islands of the Caribbean, the fine-quality, long staple Sea Island cotton grew, easily submitting itself to separation from its seed. The short staple fiber that grew inland was not as easy to work with. In 1793, Eli Whitney patented the cotton gin, which effectively separated cotton lint and seed. This mechanical development made the desire to move into the Alabama country even stronger, for many recognized this area as perfect for growing the shorter-staple crop, whose production was now practically and economically feasible.

By 1819, the newly-opened territory had enough people to apply for statehood, and on December 14 of that year, Alabama became the twenty-second state. Eleven days prior, the Alabama Territorial Legislature had incorporated two small adjacent villages, New Philadelphia and East Alabama Town, naming its new creation Montgomery. Located on the Alabama River, Montgomery developed as a trade and transportation center for Central Alabama, a region dedicated to the cultivation of cotton, often referred to as "King."

Politics, which had always intrigued some, became a matter of concern for most Montgomerians in January 1846, when the state legislature chose their home town as the third capital of the young state of Alabama. Changing from its status as a provincial market town, Montgomery now began to assume a more sophisticated air. Architecturally, Montgomery realized the prestige and importance derived from putting a proper face to the world. Its homes, churches, commercial houses, and public places reflect this awareness, especially after 1846 and the building of the capitol, which was designed by Stephen Decatur Button, a Philadelphia architect. Unfortunately, this fine edifice burned to the ground in 1849, two years after its completion. A new capitol opened on the site of the old in 1851. Ten years later, in February 1861, this capitol was the scene of the inauguration of Jefferson Davis, as Montgomery became the first capital of the Confederate States of America, a position it held for three months.

During most of the Civil War, the city supported the Confederacy with men, money, and materials, but was spared intrusion by Union troops. However, in April 1865, the war came to town with the arrival of Wilson's Raiders, a Federal cavalry force whose mission was to destroy the war-making capabilities of Alabama, whatever they might be. Hours before the Federal forces arrived, the city council, in concurrence with the departing Confederate troops, burned the thousands of bales of cotton stored in local warehouses so that they would not fall into Federal hands. According to contemporary accounts, the rising smoke obliterated the setting sun—a most appropriate picture, for not only was the sun going down on Montgomery, but on the Confederacy as well. Wilson kept tight rein on his troops, proffered protection to householders and businesses, and moved eastward in a few days. The war was over, and Montgomery was fortunate that it was not destroyed, as were Richmond and other Southern cities. Reconstruction was neither the best nor the worst of times, but a period when two racial groups had to adjust to major social, economic, and political changes. Black neighborhoods such as the affluent Centennial Hill developed, businesses opened, and African-American churches acted as both academic institutions and religious training grounds.

With Reconstruction behind, the Montgomery of the 1880s was a prosperous, energetic town, relishing the improving economy and taking great delight in modern conveniences. First came the telephone in 1881, and two years later came electric lights. "Jingle Bells," a mule-drawn street railway, rolled through parts of town in 1885, but the next year the "Lightning Route," an electrically powered trolley, took the place of the slower streetcars. In 1887, the electrifying of all 15 miles of service brought Montgomery the distinction of being the first city in the western hemisphere to have an electric street railway system. Montgomery once again gained transportation recognition when, in 1910, the Wright brothers brought the "Wright Flyer" to town and operated a flying school for three months on the Kohn Plantation, west of the town. Many flocked to see the miraculous flights. One of the first night flights in history took place over the city in the spring of 1910.

During World War I, Camp Sheridan, an infantry training base, brought thousands of young men to the city. One such man was the novelist F. Scott Fitzgerald, who met his future wife, the local belle Zelda Sayre, at a dance at the Montgomery Country Club. Another military installation, which was to have a more far-reaching effect than the army base, was Ardmont, an air repair depot on the site of the Wright flying school. From this rather humble beginning developed Maxwell Field and the mighty Air University of today.

When the Depression ravaged America's cities, Montgomery was not immune to the pain, but it did not suffer to the same degree as did other cities, including its sister, Birmingham. With an agriculturally-based economy, the seat of government for the state, and a strong military presence at Maxwell Field, the city managed to hold its course. While banks were failing all over the country, only one financial house, the Fourth National Bank, went under in Montgomery.

World War II brought thousands of strangers in for training, but this time it was not an infantry camp but two air bases, Maxwell and Gunter Fields, where cadets received flying instructions. Even prior to the entry of the war by the United States, British and French flyers were stationed at Gunter; unfortunately, some lost their lives while here, and an area of Oakwood Cemetery contains the graves of those who died.

In 1955 and 1956, Montgomery received worldwide attention with the start of the Bus Boycott, which began because of the treatment black citizens received on public transportation. Seating arrangements, lack of black drivers in minority neighborhoods, and the rudeness of some white operators were the immediate grievances which precipitated the refusal of Rosa Parks, a seamstress and secretary of the NAACP, to give up her seat to a white person on the evening of December 1, 1955. Her arrest was the trigger which set the boycott in motion and placed a young minister, Dr. Martin Luther King, on a path which would bring him the Nobel Peace Prize and cut short his life by assassination.

Montgomery, riverport for King Cotton and the first capital of the Confederacy, was also the birthplace of the modern civil rights movement. Coming to terms with the dichotomy of its past has not always been easy, but the city has a certain easygoing, somewhat rural flavor, which lends a tolerance to her people. Through photographs depicting the changing scenes at corners in Alabama's capital city, this book will relate small portions of the town's story, past, and present.

One

Montgomery, County and City

Noted as the best lands in the Creek Cession, those in proximity to the Big Bend in the Alabama River seemed destined for important use; included in this estimation was Montgomery County. Organized in 1816, it originally covered more territory than the map below indicates, for the state legislature often carved new counties from portions of existing ones. The county bears the name of Lemuel Montgomery, a young lawyer from Nashville, who was with Andrew Jackson at Horseshoe Bend and who was one of his favorite soldiers. Montgomery died storming the barricade placed by the Creeks as a defense against American soldiers.

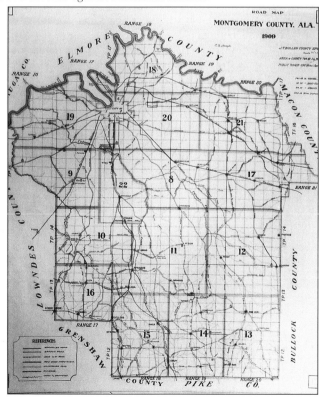

Map of Montgomery County.

Andrew Dexter. When land sales opened in Milledgeville, Georgia, in August 1817, eager buyers were on hand. Among them was General John Scott, a Virginian who had moved into the Broad River region of central Georgia, prospering as both a planter and a businessman. As agent for a group of investors who saw the potential for making money on the new frontier, he bought a quarter-section of land on a bluff of the Alabama River. Another purchaser was a Massachusetts lawyer, Andrew Dexter, who arrived at the sale with enough inherited Revolutionary War scrip to make an initial investment of five percent down on a quarter-section east of Scott's property, but not adjacent to the river. Others participating in the sale included William Graham, a North Carolinian who invested in land south of Dexter's. (Portrait in Montgomery City Hall.)

John Scott. Scott and his fellows founded Alabama Town on the bluff. Dexter, arranging with a new acquaintance, John Falconer, to assist in paying for his lands, had them surveyed and began selling lots in the village he named New Philadelphia. This town flourished while Scott's, unable to attract traders and merchants, languished. Failing in his original efforts, Scott and other parties purchased land immediately west of Dexter's and laid out a site they named East Alabama Town. Unlike their earlier attempts, this village prospered, competing with New Philadelphia for settlers who were arriving in such numbers throughout the Alabama Territory that by the closing months of 1819, it was obvious that the population was sufficient for statehood. (Portrait in Murphy House, Montgomery Water and Sewer Board.)

William Wyatt Bibb (left) and Richard Montgomery (right). The leaders of the two towns soon reached the conclusion that competition was detrimental and that consolidation would benefit both. Petitioning the Alabama Territorial Legislature, which was meeting to draw up plans for entering the Union, officials of the two villages suggested Montgomery as the name for the new town, honoring General Richard Montgomery, of Revolutionary War fame. On December 3, 1819, the town of Montgomery came into being; eleven days later, Alabama became the 22nd state, with William Wyatt Bibb as its first governor. In January 1820, Montgomery's first election resulted in a seven-man council which chose a leader, William Graham, from among its members. The population totaled 401. Growing with the arrival of the new settlers, the town was fulfilling the role its founders had envisioned. Dexter believed that Montgomery would be the state capital and had deeded a hill at the eastern end of Market Street to the town with instructions that it could only be given to the state when Montgomery did become the capital. In 1846, some nine years after Dexter's death from yellow fever, the legislature voted to move the government from Tuscaloosa to Montgomery. (Both images from Landmarks Collection.)

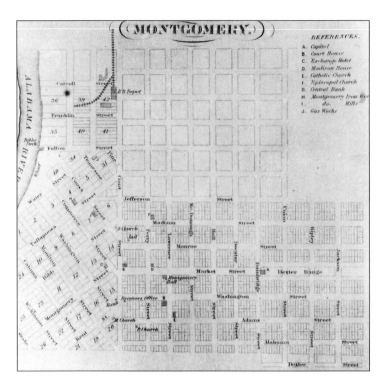

Early Street Map. Montgomery's downtown street patterns evolved from the layouts of the original villages of New Philadelphia and East Alabama Town. Dexter's plan was a grid pattern, with north-south streets named for heroes of the War of 1812, and east-west streets bearing the names of the first presidents. Scott's thoroughfares, oriented toward the river, carried names of early settlers and functions, like Commerce Street, and Indian words such as Tallapoosa. (ADAH.)

Marquis de Lafayette. Montgomery's earliest distinguished guest, Revolutionary War hero the Marquis de LaFayette, visited on April 3 and 4, 1825, on his grand tour of the United States. He was royally entertained by the excited inhabitants of the young town. Governor Israel Pickens came up from the capital, Cahaba, to extend a state welcome, and on the last night of LaFayette's stay, a ball at Freeney's Tavern concluded with the celebrants escorting him to the steamboat *Henderson* for his trip to Mobile. (Landmarks Collection.)

Two
Court Square Corners

Montgomery has been the seat of Montgomery County since 1820. The first courthouse, completed in 1822, stood near an artesian well at the western end of Market Street, the main thoroughfare of New Philadelphia. This wooden building and a later 1835 brick one served the populace until after the city became the state capital in 1846. Businesses, including those selling land, slaves, cotton, and other goods, gravitated to the square in front of the courthouse, and this practice continued after officials moved county government to the corner of Washington Avenue and Lawrence Street. Even though the courthouse is no longer on the site and the area is not truly square, it will forever be Court Square.

Burning of the Capitol, 1849. The first available view of Court Square and the town itself is a lithograph made from a daguerreotype taken by A.G. Parks, a photographer with a gallery in the Winter Building on the Square, who photographed the burning of Alabama's State Capitol on December 14, 1849. Standing in front of the courthouse or perhaps even on its steps, he captured the image of the conflagration. The four iron posts in the foreground surrounded the wooden cover of the artesian well. (An original print in Landmarks Collection.)

Northeast Court Square, Belshaw Building. Built in the early 1830s on Court Square's northeast corner, the Belshaw Building was one of the town's earliest brick commercial structures. Over the years it housed tailors, photographers, Mertieef's New Dollar Store, jewelers, a beauty salon, and a variety of offices. It may also have been a "taxi" stand, as all the buggies drawn up to the curb seem to be about the same size and type, waiting, perhaps, for customers. The unpaved streets, either muddy or dusty, stretched across the Square, and with livestock around, one can imagine the problems besetting ladies in long dresses as they moved from store to store on their shopping rounds. (Algernon Blair Collection, ADAH.)

Lehman-Durr. Behind the Belshaw Building was Lehman-Durr, a firm of cotton merchants and bankers. Immigrants from Germany, the Lehmans began their American careers as peddlers in the plantation lands of the Alabama Black Belt. By the time of the Civil War, one brother was trading in New York, and eventually the entire family moved North, where they achieved great economic success as the financial house of Lehman Brothers. The tower farther down the street was that of the First Baptist Church. The telegraph pole and gaslight in the foreground indicated two services the city had enjoyed since the antebellum era; the telegraph reached Montgomery in the late 1840s, and gaslights arrived in February of 1854. (Algernon Blair Collection.)

Moses Building, 1888. In the 1880s, Montgomery was in the midst of a building boom. Moses Brothers Banking and Realty Company, the city's largest business, acquired the valuable Belshaw property and demolished the old building to make way for the state's first "skyscraper," the six-story Moses Building topped with a pyramid-shaped tower. The building was something of an anachronism, with load-bearing masonry walls just as steel and concrete skeletal frames were beginning to appear. Fascinated with the construction, people came from miles around to watch the building rise, and upon its completion many lined up to ride the elevator, the second one in Montgomery. The first was in the 1884 Federal Building on Dexter Avenue. (1894 *Art Works/* Landmarks Collection.)

McGehee Brothers, Moses Building, c. 1895. The drug firm of McGehee Brothers did business at 15 North Court Street from an elegantly detailed storefront that was complete with stained glass. The young man with the bicycle promised speedy delivery of all customers' drug needs. Handsome though it was, within a few years the Moses Building was as out of date as had been the Belshaw Building. (Landmarks Collection.)

First National Bank Building, 1907.
In 1891, the Moses Brothers went bankrupt; as a result, the Moses Building became the property of W.F. Vandiver. In 1907, Vandiver swapped buildings with the First National Bank, which occupied a six-story building a few doors down Commerce Street. When Vandiver announced his intentions to add two more stories to his new office, First National Bank officials decided to tear the Moses Building down and build new headquarters. By this time, the steel-framed skyscraper had proven its worth nationally, and bank officials decided to construct one in Montgomery. The new building was ready for occupancy by October 1907. One of the bank's many customer services was a special department for ladies, proclaiming that "Women Make Good Bank Customers." (Collier/Landmarks Collection.)

Lion's Head, 1996. In the mid-1970s, the First Alabama Bank (formerly First National) renovated its exterior walls and placed mechanical elements on the roof behind a towering "bonnet." To commemorate its past, the bank placed four of the lions' heads that had originally adorned the cornice on a pylon in the plaza created when the City redirected the flow of traffic through the Square. (Ken Reynolds, photographer/Landmarks Collection.)

Northwest Court Square, Exchange Hotel, c. 1874. In 1846, a group of businessmen constructed the Exchange Hotel at the corner of Commerce and Montgomery Streets on the site of one of the town's earliest hostelries, the Mansion House. Designed by Stephen Decatur Button, architect for Montgomery's first capitol building, the Greek Revival Exchange Hotel became the political and social center of the city. When the capitol burned, the legislature moved into the hotel and almost uninterruptedly continued its debates. The best hotel in town, the Exchange offered amenities such as a fine dining room and comfortable private rooms. Its clientele as well as townspeople could also take pleasure and comfort in an 1850s city ordinance decreeing that no longer could hotels, restaurants, and private dwellings toss their noxious wastes into the streets. During the organization of the Confederacy and in the early days of the Civil War, the hotel swarmed with people seeking offices or carrying on the business of the new government. Until their house on Bibb Street was ready, President and Mrs. Jefferson Davis lived at the Exchange. (Algernon Blair Collection/Scott Photographic Services.)

Exchange Hotel, Visit of President Grover Cleveland, 1887. Excitement reigned on October 20, 1887, when President Grover Cleveland came for a one-day visit during a swing through the South. The town had cleaned, painted, and decorated every public building in preparation for the grand event. People came by special trains from all over the state to welcome Cleveland, the first Democrat elected to the presidency since the Civil War. His dedicated followers fully agreed with the *Daily Dispatch*, which announced that "The Democratic Rooster Crows Unusually Loud Today." After a parade up Commerce Street from the train station, the chief executive spoke from the balcony of the Exchange Hotel. The parade then continued out to the Fairgrounds near the Alabama River where the State Fair was in progress; Cleveland again addressed the crowds before returning to the city and taking a late afternoon train for Atlanta. (ADAH.)

New Exchange Hotel. In 1905, owners decided to tear down the Old Exchange and build in its place the New Exchange, a modern, up-to-date facility. For many years, it, too, served as a social and political hub, but by the mid-1970s, both it and its reputation had suffered the ravages of time. With motels replacing hotels as popular overnight accommodations, and the night life of the city center declining, the obsolete building disappeared from the Square in 1974. (Collier/Landmarks Collection.)

Colonial Company, 1996. The demolition of the New Exchange left a serious hole in the fabric of the Square, but in 1984/85, the Colonial Company built a handsome polished granite and glass building where the proud Exchange hotels once stood.(Ken Reynolds, photographer.)

Crommelin Block, c. 1850s. The removal of the courthouse in 1852 made room for businesses on the west side of the Square. The Crommelin Block, a row of two-story structures, housed an architect, an auction house, a dry goods emporium, and grocery stores. Although the city had suffered from a lack of supplies during the Civil War, by the time of this photograph, conditions were improving, with steamboats, a few trains, and wagons once again bringing goods and foodstuffs for grocers to offer to their customers. (ADAH.)

Cotton Market, c. 1905. Large, imposing buildings had replaced the small original structures at the turn of the century along the west side of the Square. In 1901, local architect Frank Lockwood designed the handsome Capitol Clothing Store, which catered to the male population, while Alex Rice was a department store for men and women. A typical late fall Court Square scene centered around farmers and their cotton-laden wagons awaiting bids from cotton merchants, who sampled the staple by slashing through the bales with sharp knives, pulling out a handful of fiber, giving it a cursory grading and offering a price. Upon completion of sales, merchants stored the bales in warehouses until shipping time. Well into the twentieth century, cotton formed the base of Montgomery's economy with its merchants, warehouses, compresses, and transportation facilities all bringing in their share of the revenue. (Philadelphia Museum of Art.)

Liggett Drugstore, 1950s. Liggett Drugstore occupied the ground floor of the former Capitol Clothing Store. With a popular lunch and soda fountain, it often provided customers with food and drink while they awaited the city buses that stopped on the corner of Montgomery Street and Court Square. Down Montgomery Street was the ladies' favorite shop, Al Levy's, and beyond that towered the Bell Building. Just south of the drugstore, the Strand Theater brought Hollywood to Montgomery with first-rate movies. (Scott Photographic Services.)

One Court Square. In the 1960s, urban renewal left its scar on Court Square with the demolition of a whole city block of buildings which were replaced by One Court Square, a large office complex and parking deck. The block then took on a completely new character, but the fountain remained intact, for as the symbol of the city since 1885, no one dared to touch it. (Landmarks Collection.)

21

Victory Celebration, 1919. On May 12, 1919, all Montgomery turned out to welcome the 167th Rainbow Division home from the First World War, the "war that was to make the world safe for democracy." Banners hung from every pole and post, triumphant arches stretched across Dexter Avenue and Commerce Street, and Court Square Fountain, dazzling in greenery and patriotic colors, beckoned the crowd. The decorative arrangements included a wooden deck

that covered Big Basin, where a band played lustily over the excited voices of men, women, and children. Decked out in their springtime best, the crowd anticipated the great moment when the men marched up from Union Station. Beyond the fountain, on the west side of the Square, was the Orpheum Theater and a variety of stores and shops. (ADAH.)

Big Basin, 1867. In 1853, the City dug out the Court Square artesian well, creating "Big Basin," which the citizens hoped would supply sufficient water for fighting fires and watering stock. This photograph of firemen and interested spectators in all probability was taken at the Firemen's Parade of June 13, 1867. The "fire laddies" performed many amazing feats of skill and daring, including scaling the Exchange Hotel and competing to see which engine company could first work up steam and "throw water." The photographer, possibly F.A. Gerrish, took this picture looking south across the Square. (ADAH.)

South Court Square, 1874. A few years later, another photographer shot a view looking south but from a slightly different angle, including more of the verandas of the Winter Building, the large structure on the left. Behind the buildings on the right was the tower of the Court Street Methodist Church, which was designed by C.C. Ordeman, a German immigrant who worked as an architect in Montgomery during the early 1850s. Crisscrossing wheel tracks indicated the free flow of traffic in the area and the hazards both riders and pedestrians faced in setting foot onto this expanse of unpaved street. (ADAH.)

24

Hay Wagon, c. 1880. Farmers brought in wagonloads of hay for sale on the Square in this 1880 photograph, which looked south down South Court Street. Behind the buildings on the right was the new steeple of the renovated Court Street Methodist Church. (ADAH.)

South Court Square, 1950s. By the 1950s, many changes had occurred. Paved streets and sidewalks linked the sides of the Square, and different businesses lined the western side of South Court Street, including loan companies, furniture stores, cafes, and the well-known Electrik Maid Bakery. One of the city's largest residential buildings, the Walter Bragg Smith Apartments was a new and fashionable place to live, up the street from the columned Post Office and Federal Court House. In 1967, the tragic Dale's Penthouse fire atop the apartment building claimed the lives of several prominent Montgomerians. (Collier/ Landmarks Collection.)

Winter Building, c. 1880. One of Montgomery's early three-story brick structures, the Winter Building dates from the early 1840s. Built by Georgian John Gano Winter for a branch of his St. Mary's Bank, at the time of the Civil War it housed a clothing store, daguerrean gallery, professional offices, and the Magnetic Telegraph Company. From the Winter Building in April 1861, the Confederate government sent the telegram to its forces in South Carolina empowering them to remove the Federal troops from Fort Sumter, an order which started the Civil War. Later, as war news came in over the wires, operators read the results of battles and their casualties to an anxious public gathered in the Square below the galleries. (ADAH.)

Winter Building Plaque. This plaque, donated by a local patriotic group and mounted in the lobby of the Winter Building, commemorates its significant role at the start of hostilities between North and South. Now restored, the Winter Building valiantly continues to guard its Capital City corner. (Collier/Landmarks Collection.)

Central Bank, c. 1870. In 1855, the Central Bank of Alabama's president, William Knox, hired architect Stephen Decatur Button, the designer of Montgomery's first capitol, to plan a building for his thriving enterprise at the northeast corner of Market Street and Court Square. Expressing the current Renaissance Revival fashion, Button utilized ideas from fifteenth-century Venetian palaces while incorporating newly developed cast-iron decorative elements on the facade. Note the gaslights at the front entrance and at the corner. The Central Bank was the first to lend money to the Confederate government, and at the end of the war went into receivership. Later, other financial institutions occupied the building into the early years of the twentieth century. Next door was Blount's Drugstore, with a mortar and pestle ornament signifying its business. (ADAH/McEachern Collection.)

By the 1890s, the corner had gained some sophistication with more stylish buildings and electric lights, but gaslights still illuminated the front entrance of what became Farley's National Bank. The door on the side led into another financial house, the Merchants and Planters Bank. (ADAH.)

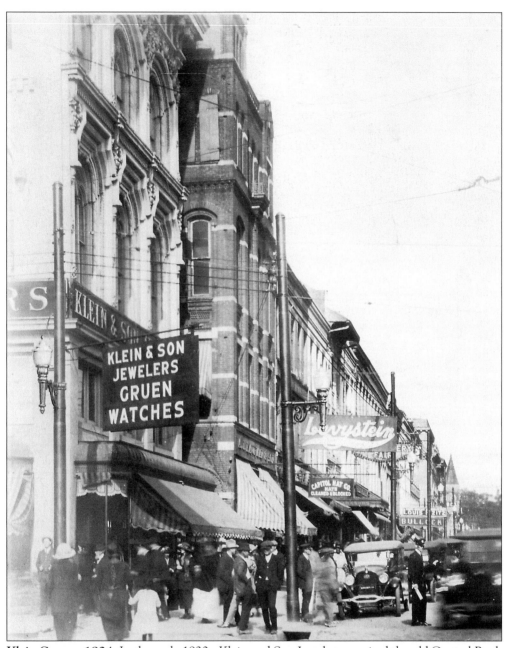

Klein Corner, 1924. In the early 1920s, Klein and Son Jewelers acquired the old Central Bank building and modified its windows and interiors. Inside, shoppers found magic and beauty in the dark-stained wooden cases where diamonds' prismatic rays radiated in the changing light, flat silver gleamed, and fine china and crystal encouraged young brides to continue the elegant table-setting traditions handed down from one generation to the next. (Landmarks Collection.)

Bank Corner and Trolley, c. 1900. Even though the men were wearing coats, this must have been a summer scene, because the open-car trolley was only in use during the hot months of the year. The Montgomery Street Railway was one of several companies that operated trolleys between 1886 and 1936. Because trolley lines went to Cloverdale, the growing suburb south of town was attracting many residents who found they could enjoy life away from the inner city. (ADAH.)

Klein Corner, 1940s. In the 1930s, Klein and Son purchased a large street clock, placing it at the corner of Dexter Avenue and North Court Street. It soon became the official time piece for all of downtown. Behind Klein's was the Montgomery Fair, the city's largest department store where clothes, cosmetics, candy, linens, housewares, gifts, and books provided hours of shopping or leisurely browsing for several generations of central Alabamians. Businessmen and shoppers met over bowls of hot soup and chicken salad sandwiches, enjoying the food and catching up on the news, particularly in the 1940s with word from the battlefield during World War II. (ADAH.)

Court Square, 1872. When the City dug out the artesian well, it created a basin and surrounded it with a decorative iron fence. Drivers watered their stock and firefighters filled their buckets from what citizens referred to as the "Artesian Basin," or "Big Basin." Peddlers hawked their wares and auctioneers barked prices as goods exchanged hands around this important city site. (Algernon Blair Collection.)

Central Square, 1885. In the 1880s, as the city enjoyed its prosperity, W.W. Screws, editor of the *Montgomery Advertiser*, expressed his disgust and dismay at the condition of "Big Basin," calling regularly for improvement to the "hog-wallow in the Square." Littered with trash, it had become a major eyesore and noxious factor when the city council in the summer of 1885 dispatched Alderman Carr to purchase a fountain for the site. It was with excitement that Carr wired Mayor Warren S. Reese that, having acquired a fountain, he hoped it would please the town. In September, the elements arrived, along with an installation supervisor from the J.L. Mott Iron Works, the New York firm which manufactured the base and its ornaments. (ADAH.)

The Lightning Route, 1887. In 1886, the Capital City Street Railway electrified one line of streetcars. Known as the Lightning Route because it could move 6 miles an hour, uphill and down, the trolley gave impetus to the development of the suburbs and public parks away from the inner city. In 1887, in a daring move, the company inaugurated electric service on its entire 15-mile system, thus becoming the first all-electric operation in the western hemisphere. This picture, taken by S.P. Tresslar, possibly dates from the day the system first went into service. (ADAH.)

The Lightning Route, 1936. After fifty years of providing reliable service, the Lightning Route made its last run on March 8, 1936. Throngs gathered in the Square, with much reminiscing about putting pennies on the tracks, greasing the rails with soap, hanging onto the rear of the cars while on roller skates, going to school, to work, to the parks, to ball games, to church and, of course, courting. Miss Toccoa Cozart, one of the first women to ride the electric trolley, was on board for that last nostalgic trip. In all probability there were a few tears shed for an era that had come to an end. (Roton Collection.)

Court Square in the Snow, 1901. An unusual scene in Montgomery, a light snow covered the ground in this 1901 view across Court Square. A few hardy souls ventured out, bundled up and walking with heads down to avoid the wind, while two mules with lowered heads stood forlornly near Big Basin. Trolley riders, less exposed than pedestrians, still had to face the cold. Tenants in the proud Moses Building had no inkling that in a few short years their office would be gone, a victim of progress. The venerable bank building (right) and the fountain remain today, the only two structures from this picture that are still standing. (Library of Congress.)

Court Square in the Sun, 1905. This postcard of Court Square in the sun invited sender and recipient to the Capital City to ride the trolley, to view the fountain, to shop along Dexter Avenue and, of course, to visit the capitol. (Oglesby Collection.)

32

Three

Monroe Street Corners

James Monroe, fifth president of the United States, was in office at the time of Montgomery's founding; Andrew Dexter named a street in his honor, as he had done for the previous four presidents. Monroe Street was a meeting place for people from all walks of life, and its sights, sounds, smells, and syncopation made it a very unique place within the life of the town.

City Hall, c. 1890. Upon becoming the state capital, Montgomery began to create a new urban image for itself, and a proper city hall became essential. At the northwest corner of Monroe and North Perry Streets, the City built a hall which served until the late 1860s. The building eventually became an imposing structure with a city market on the ground level where vendors rented stalls for the sale of meats, fish, fresh produce, and other goods. The next floor housed the municipal administrative offices. On the third was a large auditorium which provided space for many activities, including a place for lady bicyclists to practice in private before venturing out into public as the new biking craze swept the land. (ADAH.)

City Hall, Fire and Police Headquarters, c. 1900. Police and fire headquarters and stables, housed in city hall, extended along North Perry and rounded the corner onto Madison. For years, volunteer fire units admirably protected Montgomery, but in 1898 the City assumed full responsibility for the critical service. The City had long provided policemen. The photographer shot this photo looking west on Madison, with the steeple of the First Baptist Church in the background. (ADAH.)

Montgomery Grays Headquarters, c. 1890. From the Civil War to the eve of World War I, the Montgomery Grays were a prominent volunteer militia unit that attracted young men for patriotic, military, and social purposes. The company had its elaborate headquarters in city hall and departed from there for trips to other parts of the country where they competed with similar organizations for awards in military drills and routines. (ADAH.)

Theater Programs. City hall's auditorium was the setting for concerts and plays, with well-known artists and actors frequently appearing there. Among those performing in 1922 were soprano Claire Dux and violinist Jascha Heifetz. Four years later, noted violinist Fritz Kreisler gave a recital in the hall. (Landmarks Collection.)

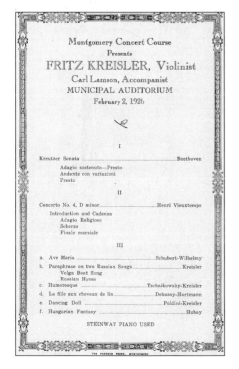

City Hall Fire, 1932. During the early evening hours of March 21, 1932, a deadly fire completely destroyed city hall, and with it many valuable municipal records and documents were lost. An aerial view taken on March 22 recorded the tragedy of the previous evening,

illustrating the hull of the building in the center of the photograph. The church steeple on the left was that of St. John's, and the Greek Revival house beyond that was the Pollard Mansion, demolished in the late 1930s. (Copy of photograph in Landmarks Collection.)

Smoldering Ruins, March 1932. This snapshot, taken from the second floor of the old Montgomery Theater building across the street, depicts the ruins of the Monroe Street facade of city hall. Huge crowds gathered at the scene, and people who lived several miles from town recalled seeing the flames against the night sky. The *Montgomery Advertiser* noted the grave concern of officials at the time that this wall would collapse onto the large crowd of onlookers. (Landmarks Collection.)

Clean-up. Soldiers from Maxwell Field, the local military base, and inmates from the city and county jails assisted in fighting the city hall flames. As the clean-up got underway, prisoners clad in stripes helped remove debris from the site. (Landmarks Collection.)

New City Hall. The current city hall, designed by Frank Lockwood Jr., dates from 1936/37, with financing a cooperative effort between the City and the Federal Works Progress Administration. Algernon Blair, Inc., a noted local firm, was the general contractor.

City Hall. The City formally dedicated the building with great fanfare on September 30, 1937. (Collier/Landmarks Collection.)

Montgomery Theater Interior, 1888. On the southwest corner of Monroe and North Perry Streets, businessman Charles T. Pollard built the Montgomery Theater in 1860. One of the first actors to perform there was John Wilkes Booth, who appeared for a week soon after the theater's opening, playing in *Hamlet*, *Richard III*, and *Romeo and Juliet*. Another event of lasting importance was the introduction to the local bandmaster, Herman Arnold, of a minstrel tune that he transcribed for the Montgomery Brass Band. A few months later this band led the inaugural parade of Jefferson Davis while playing the jaunty tune "Dixie." Being ideally located on the railroad between New Orleans and Atlanta, Montgomery had the opportunity to see many of the leading thespians and musicians of the late nineteenth century. Until its closing in 1907, the Montgomery Theater was the city's palace of entertainment. In this 1888 city promotional booklet, the artist richly depicts the theater's interior following a mid-1880s renovation. (From 1888 booklet, Dexter Avenue Methodist Collection.)

Playbill from November 1, 1898. (James/Landmarks Collection.)

South Side, Monroe Street, 1950s. Since the Montgomery Theater closed in 1907, a number of department stores have been located in the building; for the past three decades or more Webber's has been the occupant. Photographer Franklin Collier focused his camera along the south side of Monroe Street for this unusually still and quiet view of the normally bustling thoroughfare. (Collier/Landmarks Collection.)

Webber's Department Store, 1990s. A historic marker pays tribute to the grand old building's interesting past, but it does not relate an oft-told story regarding the management's having reserved one section of the gallery for ladies of the neighborhood who frequented the streets. Today, the walls of now-unused upper floors still bear shadows of the theater's galleries and stage area. (Landmarks Collection.)

Corner, Monroe and North Perry. A photographer stood on the roof of city hall to snap this photograph of a small trolley nosing its way toward the corner of Monroe and North Perry Streets about 1890. Some seventy years later, Franklin Collier photographed the same location, but from a lower angle. While some of the buildings are the same, the mode of transportation had been radically altered.

Monroe Corners. Collier then turned his camera eastward on Monroe toward its intersection with North Lawrence Street, where a prominent black business district included the Pekin Cafe, the Pekin Theater, the Pekin Pool Room, and shops. A parking deck now covers the Monroe Street block between North Perry and North Lawrence. (Collier/Landmarks.)

Burke's Corner, North Court and Monroe Streets. After the Civil War, Monroe Street became a retail center with peddlers, stores, and cafes offering goods and services sometimes nearly impossible to obtain elsewhere in town. Burke's Drugstore carried a wide selection of merchandise and served all segments of the population with its motto: "If you love us, you will smile." (Collier/Landmarks Collection.)

Burke's Corner, 1940s. Photographer David Savlar recorded a familiar scene at Burke's corner, where farmers and urbanites jostled each other on the crowded sidewalks. Saturday was a particularly busy day, as people from the country came to town to shop, visit, and indulge themselves and their children with treats not always available in rural areas. (Savlar Collection.)

Tatum's Fish Market, Next Door to Burke's, 1950s. Suspended from the sidewalk overhang, fish logos advertised the merchandise for sale. Mixed with the aroma of the fish were those of fresh and not-so-fresh fruits and vegetables sold from old wagons parked against the curb (seen below). (Joe Holloway Jr., photographer, Holloway/Landmarks Collection.)

Tom's Ready to Wear, 1950s. Tom's stood on the east side of Tatum's Fish Market, whose sign enumerated the variety of seafood stocked, including oysters. Montgomery's appetite for oysters was legendary, and nineteenth-century editors of the *Advertiser* often commented on the excitement a shipment generated around town and the enjoyment derived from eating them. Reflected in the store windows was the scene across the street on Monroe's north side. (Collier/Landmarks Collection.)

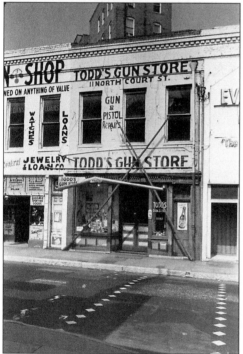

(Left) Todd's Gun Store, 1950s. At the foot of Monroe Street, facing North Court Street, was Todd's Gun Store, the oldest continuing enterprise in Montgomery. Founded in the early 1820s on Commerce Street by a Prussian gunsmith, Nicholas Becker, the firm moved to the south side of Dexter Avenue in the 1880s and subsequently to this site. Later, the business relocated farther down North Court Street. (Collier/Landmarks.) **(Right) Alabama Bancshares.** On the site where Burke's once stood, the Alabama Bancshares building added a touch of modern architectural style to the older structures which are still in abundance on this block of Monroe. (Ken Reynolds, photographer.)

City Pawn Shop, 1950s. Photographer Franklin Collier continued his cataloging of local scenes on the north side of Monroe Street. Across from Tom's Ready to Wear was the City Pawn Shop, located in the 1870s Sutter Building. Other businesses housed in similar older structures lined this western end of Monroe Street.

Cathcart-Rogers. Note the adornment on the roof of the Cathcart-Rogers Furniture Co. A parking deck is now on the site of these structures. (Collier/Franklin.)

Monroe Street, West. With his camera set up in the alley, photographer Joe Holloway Jr. recorded three shoppers on a sunlit day. (Holloway/Landmarks Collection.)

Monroe Street, East. While the western end of Monroe Street was commercial, the eastern blocks were residential until the state acquired the property for governmental use. Franklin Collier, standing on the capitol roof, noted a neighborhood ambience which was to last only a few more years. (Collier/Landmarks Collection.)

Four

Dexter Avenue Corners

Dexter Avenue, originally Market Street, was the main thoroughfare of New Philadelphia. The first cabins and storehouses were along the eastern end of the street, near the knoll originally called Goat Hill (later Capitol Hill). After the merger of New Philadelphia and East Alabama Town, settlers gravitated westward, closer to Court Square, the artesian well, and their new fellow-townsmen. Market Street flourished as a retail center and a vibrant part of the developing metropolis. When Montgomery became the state capital in 1846, the new state house became the road's crowning glory. In 1884, the city council changed the name of Market Street to Dexter Avenue in honor of town founder Andrew Dexter.

Montgomery Hall Painting, 1840. Built in 1835, the Montgomery Hall soon earned the praise of English traveler and lecturer James Buckingham, who commented that his accommodations were "excellent" and the hotel as good as any in Boston. In 1842, ex-president Martin Van Buren was a guest. Seven years later, another ex-president, James K. Polk, visited. Architect Charles Ordeman renovated the hotel in 1851, and a decade later it hosted Confederate government personnel. During military Reconstruction, Federal officials were lodgers, and the proprietor, when called upon to pay back taxes, complained that she could if she were able to collect rent from those same tenants. (ADAH.)

Sketch, Corner of Market and South Perry Streets. On the left is the 1830s Pond Building where Lewis Pond operated his cash store. The building on the right, dating from the 1840s, traditionally housed druggists and physicians who often noted their location as at the "Sign of the Eagle." Mounted on a fluted column, the gilded bird adorned the corner for many years. (ADAH.)

Market Street Lithograph, 1857. Market Street was the principal street of the growing, prosperous capital city of the leading cotton-producing state in the South. Although sporting sophisticated urban architecture, the town still retained its agricultural character, with mule- and oxen-drawn wagons and a dray loaded with cotton headed around the newly-opened Artesian Basin. On pillars and posts along the avenue are the "logos" of the period advertising the businesses located within; note the cobbler's boot on the left and the druggist's lion and mortar on the right. (Original from *Harper's Weekly*.)

Firemen's Celebration, 1867. On June 13, 1867, in the midst of Reconstruction's "hard times," the volunteer fire companies provided the town with entertainment as they paraded, demonstrated their skills at "throwing water," and scaled the Exchange Hotel. These festivities brought pleasure, excitement, and color into the lives of those still recovering from the pains of war and concluded with an award ceremony around the Artesian Basin in Court Square. The Grey Eagle Company No. 3 was in the foreground; they had received high praise for saving the town from flames when city authorities burned the cotton to prevent its falling into the hands of Union troops. Photographer F.A. Gerrish took the picture from the roof of Molton's Store, at the corner of Court Square and Montgomery Street. (ADAH.)

Montgomery Hall, 1880. Past its prime and in deteriorating condition, the Montgomery Hall faced demolition to make way for the United States Courthouse and Post Office. Livestock often drank from the Houston Fountain, placed at the intersection in 1874 to honor the newly-elected governor, George Smith Houston, and to celebrate a return to "home rule" as Reconstruction came to an end in Alabama. (ADAH.)

Frank Leslie's *Weekly*, **November 1874.** In the summer of 1874, throngs gathered on Montgomery streets to receive rations sent by the Federal government to ease the suffering caused by devastating spring floods throughout the South and East. On March 21, the *Montgomery Advertiser* reported that "Perfect crowds of people stand at the foot of Commerce Street all day long to muse over the six continuous miles of water spread out before them." Railroad tracks and bridges washed away and crops had to be re-planted, some twice. People lost

homes, livestock, and possessions. On May 18, Alabama's delegation in the House of Representatives pushed through a resolution authorizing the president to "issue rations and clothing to the inundated destitute of the Tombigbee, Warrior and Alabama rivers. The passage required considerable personal urging." (*Montgomery Advertiser*, May 19, 1874, Landmarks Collection.)

Federal Courthouse and Post Office, Dexter and South Lawrence Streets, 1884. Lewis Owen, jeweler and builder, supervised the construction of this building, which opened in 1884. The Alabama stone used in its foundation was of such quality that the *Advertiser* of March 21, 1882, pronounced it the finest in the world. One of the immensely popular aspects of the courthouse was the elevator, the first such device in Montgomery. (ADAH.)

Upper Dexter, c. 1888. Mr. A.L. Clapp, president of Curbow and Clapp Marble Company, drove his horse "Friday" past his place of business on the north side of upper Dexter Avenue, adjoining Nix Marble Yard. Stone masons and retailers, Curbow and Clapp performed much of the work on the Confederate Memorial on the grounds of the Alabama State Capitol. (ADAH.)

Upper Dexter, 1891. J.N. Curbow and A.L. Clapp expanded their business with the construction of a handsome building at the old Nix Marble Yard site on the north side of upper Dexter. (ADAH.)

Dexter Avenue, 1893. Hebe, the fountain's crowning goddess, seemed almost entangled among Dexter Avenue's myriad wires, which proclaimed the progressive nature of Montgomery as telephones, telegraphs, electric lights, and trolleys all required special lines to deliver their services. (ADAH.)

Looking East on Dexter, Near Corner of Lawrence and Dexter, c. 1894. Streetcar tracks led directly up Dexter Avenue to the capitol through newly-planted trees, put in to enhance and improve the upper reaches of the street which had often received criticism for its shabby appearance—after all, this was the "Capital City." The City paved Dexter Avenue with vitrified brick in 1895, further improving its appearance and condition. On the upper left is the Dexter Avenue Methodist Church with an unfinished steeple, indicating the financial troubles brought on by the Panic of 1893, a nationwide depression caused by several factors including severe agricultural problems and a drain on gold reserves.

Dexter from Above, c. 1906. This view of the entire stretch of Dexter Avenue could only have been taken from the twelve-story Bell Building, one of the city's first skyscrapers, which was then under construction. The Montgomery Fair Department Store had begun a new building, and while this was underway, the management used part of the old Central Bank building for its merchandising.

Trolley Problems, November 23, 1906. The electric trolley, the "Lightning Route," changed the face of Montgomery by providing transportation to and from the central city, permitting the development of suburbs. Initially, both races rode, with black riders in the rear and white riders toward the front of the cars. However, in 1896, the U.S. Supreme Court ruled in the *Plessy* vs. *Ferguson* case that accommodations on trains should be separate but equal. Ten years later, the Montgomery City Council passed an ordinance requiring the local trolley line to put on separate cars for black passengers. The company, unwilling to take on the extra expense, failed to comply, and on the morning of November 23, police arrested drivers as they arrived with their morning passengers on Dexter Avenue. Also taken into custody were the officials of the Montgomery Traction Company, operator of the street railway. Trolleys lined Dexter, bringing transportation to a halt for several hours until a city court issued an injunction against the city council, requiring that service be restored. The company did not put on the additional cars, and the practice of blacks in the back and whites in front continued for another fifty years. (ADAH.)

North Side, Dexter Avenue, 1907. Built on Dexter Avenue in 1906, this building was the headquarters of the Montgomery Light and Water Power Company, which obviously believed in advertising varied sources of energy for its customers. (ADAH.)

Dexter Avenue, Western End, 1907. A picture postcard presented a panoramic view of the town. The Winter Building was in the right foreground, with the bank building on the left. The large structure with the tower was the courthouse, and behind it was St. Peter's Catholic Church. The photographer probably was on the top of the new First National Bank. (Crook Collection.)

Dexter Avenue, 1924. A series of photographs depict a busy Dexter Avenue crowded with shoppers and traffic. The three images on this page illustrate the hustle and bustle of the Capital City's most important retail district. The picture on the right, taken from midway up the block on the north side, looked toward Court Square with Silver's Five and Dime, Kress, and Pizitz in the foreground.

These photographs were on the south side of the street, illustrating a significant difference in shopping then and now. The women were all wearing hats, and probably some had on gloves, for it was not proper to go "downtown" without them. (Landmarks Collection.)

Dexter Avenue Night Scene, c. 1940. Franklin Collier took this dramatic night photograph from the corner of South Perry and Dexter Avenue at mid-century. Kress Five and Dime, the Exchange Hotel, Capitol Clothing, and the Varsity proclaimed their names proudly and prominently, as a city bus headed for Cloverdale. (Collier/Landmarks Collection.)

Dexter Avenue Night Scene, c. 1940. Photographer Franklin Collier spotted a window-shopper strolling along a quiet, dark Dexter Avenue. (Collier/Landmarks Collection.)

Five

The Capitol Corner

Following the burning of Montgomery's first capitol on December 14, 1849, discussion ensued as to whether or not the city should continue to serve as the seat of state government. While other cities would have happily assumed the role, Montgomery managed to retain the prize, and by 1851, another state house graced Goat Hill, built on the foundations of the first. Although not quite as elaborately decorated, it was a handsome Greek Revival building and appropriate to its time and place. Within ten years, destiny pushed it into the limelight as the Capitol of the Confederacy, a position far different from any previously envisioned.

Through the years the building has witnessed a grand array of events, including gubernatorial inaugurations, demonstrations for many causes, public programs, and great arrivals. The return of the 167th Division in May 1919 brought out a tremendous crowd, and in March 1965, the Selma to Montgomery Voting Rights March concluded with speeches and song on the capitol steps. On a less serious note, in June 1996, the Olympic torch, on its way to the Atlanta Games, passed in front of its colonnade.

Capitol at Montgomery, c. 1856. Based on a *c.* 1856 picture by daguerreotypist W.H. Freer, who had a studio on Market Street from 1853 to 1856, this illustration is one of the earliest known views of the capitol. (ADAH.)

Secession, 1861. With the election of Abraham Lincoln in 1860, Alabamians seriously considered the question of secession. Meeting in the capitol on January 11, 1861, delegates from around the state voted to leave the Union. The following month, representatives from seven Southern states organized the Confederate States of America in Alabama's state house, and on February 18, 1861, Jefferson Davis took the oath as president on a platform on the front portico. From February to May 1861, this building served as the headquarters of a nation until the removal of the government to Richmond, Virginia. (From *Harper's Weekly*; copy in Landmarks Collection.)

Capitol, c. 1870. A stereoscopic view of the capitol recorded the handsomely-paneled brick retaining wall and the dark terne metal dome. (McEachern Collection.)

Market Street and Capitol, c. 1870. Taken just a short distance up Market Street from the Artesian Well, this early stereoscopic view related the magnitude of the capitol as the eastern terminus of the important avenue, in essence, Alabama's main street.

Capitol, c. 1885. Street railway tracks led almost to the capitol steps and, as there were no electric lines, mules obviously still pulled the cars at the time of this photograph. White posts protected newly-planted trees put in to beautify the area from McDonough Street to Bainbridge Street. By this time, the capitol dome was white. (ADAH.)

Capitol, c. 1894. Changes were in evidence around Capitol Hill when a photographer took this picture for the 1894 edition of *Art Works,* a publication of the H.W. Kennicott Company of Chicago that recorded rural and urban scenes. Electric trolley lines hung in front of the capitol; the steps were wider and the trees were taller than in earlier photographs. (Landmarks Collection.)

View from Capitol Steps, 1906. By 1906, the trees had matured, providing a softened view and an alley in front of the capitol. This picture is from a Montgomery souvenir booklet published for S.H. Kress and Company that was among the possessions of a member of the Boys in Blue, a vaudeville company that toured this country and traveled abroad in the early years of the twentieth century. (Maurer Collection.)

Capitol Workers at 5 pm, c. 1928. By the 1920s, there was a growing force of females employed by the state. The notation on the back of this snapshot reads, "5pm. State Capitol employees leaving after day's work." (Landmarks Collection.)

The *Akron*, 1931. Gliding overhead, the Navy's airship *Akron* had a clear view of downtown Montgomery and the capitol on December 16, 1931. At this time, none of the large state buildings were in existence, and the residential character of the center city was still in evidence. (Copy print in Landmarks Collection.)

Capitol from the Air, c. 1942. As state government continued to expand, the capitol could no longer house multiple offices and departments. Employing the Birmingham architectural firm of Warren, Knight and Davis as designers, Alabama began the on-going expansion of its facilities. In 1940, the Department of Archives and History (on right) and a short time later the

Highway Department (in front and to right of capitol) were ready for the public. Both columned buildings reflected the continuing interest in Greek Revival motifs. (Copy print in Landmarks Collection.)

Folsom Inauguration, 1955. "Big Jim" Folsom, one of Alabama's best-known governors, took the oath of office for his second term on a bright January day in 1955. With Birmingham Channels 13 and 6 in attendance, this may have been the first time television cameras recorded an Alabama gubernatorial inauguration. (Collier/Landmarks Collection.)

Capitol from the Air, 1980s. Flanked by major state office buildings, the capitol presided over its domain in this 1980s aerial view of downtown Montgomery. (Alabama Bureau of Tourism and Travel.)

Six

Commerce Street Corners

The main avenue of East Alabama Town, Commerce Street led directly to the wharf and river. Originally taverns, storehouses, and residences lined the broad thoroughfare which, depending on the weather, could be very muddy or extremely dusty. Appropriately named, it served along with Market Street as one of the primary business arteries of the city.

Helping to establish Montgomery as a transportation center, the first steamboat reached the town in 1821, and thirty years later railroad entrepreneurs connected rail lines with those at West Point, Georgia, opening up train travel from the Capital City to the Northeast and Midwest. River, road, and rail carried the region's greatest crop, cotton, and goods entered the city by the same means. By the time of the Civil War, cotton warehouses lined Commerce and adjacent streets. Following the conflict, the city developed its wholesale industry to become the largest market in Central Alabama.

Commerce Street, 1870s. Looking across Court Square, the photographer of this early image of Commerce Street observed the rural-urban dichotomy of the town, with drivers of covered wagons, oxcarts, and horse-drawn carriages mingling and attending to their businesses or pleasures. The Belshaw Building is on the right in this 1870s picture. (Algernon Blair Collection.)

Old Exchange Hotel, c. 1890. On the left is another view of the Old Exchange Hotel where, following an 1885 renovation, the management announced that its boudoirs were fit for an Egyptian queen—as far as is known, no one of that lineage ever registered. In the distance down Commerce Street is "Little Basin," a more adequate supplier of water than the famous "Big Basin." (ADAH.)

Temple Building, 1874. At the northeast corner of Commerce and Bibb Streets, the Grand Masonic Lodge shared the Temple Building, a post-Civil War Second Empire structure, with LeGrand and Company. Opening with fanfare on April 15, 1874, the store chartered "horse cars" to transport people of "all ages and all sizes" who came to shop and to enjoy the music of the cornet band playing for the occasion. "Little Basin" (right foreground) was a popular source of fresh drinking water which some believed had healing qualities. (ADAH.)

Imperial Hotel, c. 1900. After LeGrand and Company moved from the Temple Building, it housed the Imperial Hotel until the great fire of June 4, 1927, destroyed it and several other buildings in the block. The conflagration was so intense and difficult to control that authorities issued a call for help from the fire departments of Prattville and Wetumpka. The photographer was looking east on Bibb Street. (ADAH.)

Confederate Office Building, c. 1900. At the northwest corner of Bibb and Commerce Streets stood the large building utilized as offices by the Confederate government during its three-month stay in Montgomery. By the turn of the century, the Pickwick Cafe, operated by members of the Ridolphi family, natives of Corsica, specialized in seafood, boasting menus including fresh oysters and a most commendable gumbo. (ADAH.)

Freeney's Tavern, c. 1890. Freeney's Tavern, built in 1824 at the southwest corner of Commerce and Tallapoosa Streets, was the city's first brick structure. On April 4, 1825, it was the site of the Grand Ball, which Montgomery and her citizens gave for the Marquis de LaFayette, who stopped for two nights on his grand tour of the country. A story often told was that the visiting Frenchman danced with every lady at the ball. The building burned in 1926. (ADAH.)

Sketch, 1886. In the fall of 1886, the *Montgomery Advertiser* published a trade and commerce issue highlighting the prosperity and progress being enjoyed by the city. To illustrate the publication, an artist detailed Commerce Street from its intersection with Tallapoosa Street southward toward Court Square. (Copy print, Landmarks Collection; newspaper, ADAH.)

Lower Commerce Street. Photographer Franklin Collier stood in the middle of Bibb and Commerce Streets in the early 1960s, one block south of the site selected by the earlier *Advertiser* artist for his 1886 rendering. Located on the bank of the Alabama River and adjacent to the railroad, Lower Commerce Street was ideally situated for the wholesale businesses which flourished there after the Civil War. At various times, businesses included a cracker factory, a work clothes factory, a machine works, and wholesalers selling all manner of goods. Unfortunately, fire frequently changed the appearance of the street. (Collier/Landmarks Collection.)

Hobbie and Teague, 1887. In the period after the Civil War, the Renaissance Revival architectural style retained its popularity, and the merchants along Commerce Street, eager to impress their customers with their worldly knowledge and means, built increasingly

handsome and stylish buildings. Hobbie and Teague, a wholesale grocery firm, was in this building in the 1880s.

Tunnel, c. 1900. A tunnel under the railroad tracks connected Lower Commerce Street to the Alabama River and its wharf. Built in 1898 as Union Station opened its doors to passengers, the tunnel's purpose was to expedite loaded drays on their trips to and from the river. The side walls of the important underpass are in the foreground. Armour and Company was in the last building on the east side of Commerce Street. Following a 1920s flood, the City closed the tunnel, but in the 1970s revitalization of the area re-opened it as a vital link to the river. (Hobbie Collection, Landmarks Foundation.)

The *Alabama*, c. 1886. Docked at the Montgomery wharf, the sternwheeler *Alabama* awaited its load of cotton for shipment to Mobile and the markets of the world. From the time the first steamboat, the *Harriett*, arrived in 1821 until the early years of the twentieth century, this was a familiar scene all along the river. (ADAH.)

Riverboats at the Wharf, c. 1900. In the upper picture, dray drivers had unloaded bales of cotton (visible in the far right), and in the lower picture, bales awaited loading for the trip downstream. (ADAH.)

Freight Depot, c. 1890. Freight clerks, men, and women gathered on the upper porch of the L&N Freight House, while drivers perched on a loaded dray below in this late nineteenth-century photograph. The Freight Depot was on Water Street, near an early passenger station. (ADAH.)

Union Station, c. 1915. With over forty passenger trains a day into Montgomery, the
L&N railroad built the handsome Union Station in 1898, complete with a 600-foot shed
to shelter travelers from the elements. Until 1979, when passenger trains stopped

coming through Montgomery, Union Station was the scene of much activity. (Postcard, Landmarks Collection.)

Schloss & Kahn.

ESTABLISHED 1871.

Wholesale Grocers

— *AND* —

Liquor Dealers.

Agents for Anheuser, Budweiser and Lemp's Bottled Beer.

ORGANIZED 1871.   **CAPITAL AND SURPLUS, $215,000**

Capital City Insurance Co.

FIRE INSURANCE.

Office, Company's Building, 35 Commerce St., MONTGOMERY.

E. B. JOSEPH,	W. D. BROWN,	P. C. SMITH,	J. S. DOWDELL,
President.	Vice-President.	Secretary.	Ass't Secretary.

Advertisements, 1893. Schloss and Kahn, a wholesale grocery firm, first opened on Commerce Street near Court Square in the 1870s. Prospering, in 1891 the company built the warehouse and office pictured in this 1893 *City Directory* advertisement. A part of the restoration efforts of the 1980s, it continues to demonstrate the ideas of the wholesale merchants who believed that a handsome building was good for business. The Capital City Insurance Company was also on Commerce Street. (Landmarks Collection.)

Commerce Street, Restoration. In the late 1970s, the preservation movement, enhanced by federal tax credits, brought about a revival of interest in restoration of commercial property in Montgomery as well as across the country. After years of decline, Commerce Street became once again a vital part of city life, as prominent professional groups and businesses met the challenge presented by the handsome, old, and neglected wholesale warehouses. The law firm of Rushton, Stakely, Johnston and Garrett was among the first to begin restoration in the area, moving into the 1891 Steiner-Lobman building. (Collier/Landmarks Collection.)

Restoration. Jackson-Thornton, an accounting firm, restored the 1894 wholesale grocery building at the same time a business consortium began work on the Old Implement Store with its unique brick designs (left). (Collier/Landmarks Collection.)

April 1, 1886. Floods frequently created havoc along Lower Commerce and other streets near the Alabama River. A very cold winter, followed by rains and thaws, created serious difficulties throughout the eastern United States in the spring of 1886. The Coosa and Tallapoosa Rivers rampaged northeast of the Capital City contributing, of course, to problems along the Alabama River, which overflowed and crested at Montgomery on April 1 at 59.7 feet. In Wetumpka, a few miles northeast of Montgomery, the waters washed away an 1840s covered bridge on the

Coosa River, while to the northwest, the Autauga Creek in Prattville severely damaged the cotton mill. These adventurous boaters were photographed on North Court, one of the flooded thoroughfares in downtown Montgomery. The river began to recede on April 2, leaving a shocked and saddened town to clean up after the debacle. (Turner Collection.)

Commerce and Water Streets, March 28, 1886. The depot on Water Street (center) and the Windsor Hotel, at the corner of Water and Commerce Streets, were awash as the full power of the Alabama River made itself known in a disastrous flood. On March 28, 1886, the *Montgomery Advertiser* noted: "Men in row boats paddled around the depot and up Commerce to the Windsor Hotel. . . ." (Turner Collection.)

Columbus Street, April 1, 1886. Two men paddled across the waters north of downtown, perhaps headed for the Alabama Warehouse, which covered the block between Columbus and Randolph, North Perry and North Court Streets. (Turner Collection.)

Seven
Residential Corners

Both East Alabama and New Philadelphia's earliest citizens lived in log cabins and often combined their living quarters with their businesses. By the 1820s, however, the town had begun to spread out with the continuous arrival of settlers, and ads in the local press for the sale of lots away from the business district encouraged people to move to higher grounds on the western ridge and the southern hills. Sawmills in the area made planed lumber available, and the use of pattern books, combined with builders' knowledge and experience, improved both the appearance and comfort of houses.

Upon becoming the state capital, Montgomery enjoyed an influx of people and ideas which stimulated a move toward the architectural trends of the larger eastern urban areas. Greek Revival, Italianate, a smattering of Second Empire, Queen Anne, shotgun houses, cottages, and, with the turn of the century, the bungalow, all these styles spread their influences across the city, as did the later Neo-Classical and multiple revival types. With no attempt to picture the entire gamut of city architecture, this chapter records just a few of the domestic treasures Montgomery has known. The vast majority of those pictured are no longer standing.

Yancey Dogtrot House, c. 1840s (Restored). Representative of a style prevalent from the settlement period, the dogtrot house allowed for both the circulation of air and the opportunity for expansion by the addition of rooms to front and rear. Originally located on the plantation of William Lowndes Yancey, lawyer, orator, and secessionist, this house is now in Old Alabama Town, a historic village in downtown Montgomery. (1894 *Art Works*, Landmarks Collection.)

Knox Hall, Built 1848; Picture 1886 (Restored). Montgomery businessman William Knox served as a member of the Capitol Building Commission in 1846. Obviously impressed with architect Stephen Button's work, Knox retained him to design a home for himself; his wife, Anna; and their fourteen children. Button designed a home quite fitting for Knox's position and for the times. The Knox family lived in the house until Mrs. Knox's death in the 1890s. Between that time and the 1920s, it was a residence, a fashionable men's club, and a "genteel" boardinghouse. In 1924, new owners built an apartment house on the front grounds, removed the massive columns, and incorporated Knox Hall into the new complex. In the 1970s, with the apartment house removed, Landmarks Foundation, Montgomery's preservation organization, purchased the house and supervised its restoration. (Landmarks Collection.)

Cowles Mansion, Built 1850s; Picture c. 1894 (Burned). Thomas Cowles, planter and railroad investor, built his Greek Revival mansion a short distance from downtown Montgomery on a bluff overlooking the Alabama River. Visitors often proclaimed it one of the finest homes in the South, noting especially the unusual scoring. As he was a promoter of and investor in railroads, it was fitting that his own home, long after his death, stood in the midst of rail yards and served as offices for the Atlantic Coast Line Railroad. In 1908, it burned, and the owners then demolished the ruins. (Algernon Blair Collection.)

Benson House, Built c. 1853; Picture c. 1894 (Demolished). Nimrod Benson was a lawyer who played an important role in the political life of Montgomery before his death from yellow fever in 1854. His home on Molton Street (corner of Church) was one of the first to break out of the symmetrical "box" and adopt the asymmetry of the Italian villas. Brick with scored plaster to resemble stone, a campanile with balconies, a bay window, and porches all combined to make this a most fashionable house for its day. (Copy print in Landmarks Collection.)

Swan-Seibels-Ball-Lanier House, Built 1855; Picture c. 1910 (Demolished). Built by entrepreneur Samuel Swan, the house became the property of John Jacob Seibels, businessman, editor, and former minister to Belgium, in 1858. The asymmetrical proportions of the house underscored the Italian villa characteristics, as did the lattice-trimmed porches and the cupola from which there were grand views of the city and surrounding countryside. (Copy print in Landmarks Collection.)

Ware-Farley-Hood House, 1850. Planter James Ware built a house with Italianate trim in the middle of the block between Adams Avenue and Alabama Street in 1850, but sold it five years later to banker James Farley, whose family lived there until after the turn of the century.

Ware-Farley-Hood House. In 1909, Horace and Susan Hood acquired this house, rolled it down the street to the corner, and "modernized" it with columns which had again become popular with the renewal of interest in classical design.

Ware-Farley-Hood House. In 1989, Landmarks Foundation moved the house to Old Alabama Town and returned it to its original appearance with cupola, wooden fretwork, and porches on three sides. It now stands on the corner of North Hull and Randolph Streets, the remaining antebellum Italianate structure to look as it did when built. (Landmarks Collection.)

Baldwin House, Built 1860, South Perry Street; Both Pictures 1870s (Demolished). Dr. W.O. Baldwin practiced medicine in Montgomery for many years and in 1860 commissioned architect John Stewart, a partner of Samuel Sloan, one of the country's best-known designers in the Italianate style. The July 10, 1860 edition of the *Montgomery Advertiser* observed that "this splendid residence will rank with the most magnificent structures in the city." In 1905, the house became headquarters for the YWCA. (Copy print in Landmarks Collection.)

Baldwin House. Handsome houses were favorite subjects of photographers when planning stereoscopic views of a city. J.H. Lakin, who came to Montgomery soon after the Civil War, took this and other scenes for the great parlor entertainer, the stereopticon, through which a double image would appear in 3-D. (McEachern Collection.)

Goetter House, c. 1880, South Court and Clayton Streets (Demolished). Joseph Goetter, merchant, chose a splendid site for his home near the crest of the Court Street hill. With the wide encircling porches, summer nights would have been delightful with family and friends looking out over the city's flickering gas lights and enjoying the breezes that played across the verandas. (1894 *Art Works*.)

Winter House, 1885, Montgomery Street (Demolished). Isaac Winter, a wholesale grocer, built his fashionable home in the 300 block of Montgomery Street in a neighborhood close to town but residential in character. Italianate details were in evidence, including the bay windows on front and side elevations, fretwork on the porch, and elaborate cornice details and brackets under the eaves. (1894 *Art Works*.)

Nicrosi-Steiner House, c. 1886 (Demolished). At the 1876 centennial celebrations, a new architectural style emerged. In a reaction to classicism and romanticism, English architects reached further back into history in an effort to bring new and refreshing approaches to style and design. Queen Anne's name, for some reason, became attached to the style, and the lady made quite a stir throughout the country; Montgomery was no exception. Incorporating almost any architectural motif, detail, material, and color, the houses demonstrated a freedom and eclecticism previously unknown. Heavily adorned with Eastlake trim, the house built by J.B. Nicrosi in 1886 on South Hull Street later became the property of R.E. Steiner, an attorney. As on many Queen Anne houses, the chimneys were major elements in the decorative scheme. (1907 *Art Works*/Landmarks Collection.)

Davidson House, c. 1890, South Court Street (Demolished). With a tower capped by a bell-shaped dome, the home of H.C. Davidson combined many different elements. The chimneys sport the tri-partite pots often associated with those in cosmopolitan European cities. (1907 *Art Works*/Landmarks Collection.)

Farley House, c. 1890 (Demolished).
Louis B. Farley, a member of the Farley Banking Company family, had a taste for the exotic, as indicated by the varying decorative elements and materials used on this house. The rounded tower with the porch offered a nice spot for someone, perhaps the master of the house, to stand for the photograph. The one chimney showing had detailed brick molding. (1894 *Art Works*/Landmark Collection.)

Thomas House, c. 1890 (Demolished).
Attorney W.H. Thomas utilized many materials—brick, granite, wood, metal, concrete, and stained and plain glass—in his home. The tall tower with arched openings was a dominant feature along South Perry Street. (1894 *Art Works*/Landmark Collection.)

South Perry Street, 1888. An unpaved, muddy street in the 1880s, Perry Street, although one of the nicest avenues in town, still held hazards for women in long skirts and dainty shoes. Young trees show the efforts underway to beautify the thoroughfare. One of the city's most prominent residential thoroughfares, South Perry Street bears the name of Commodore Oliver Hazard Perry, of War of 1812 fame. In the 1850s, it gained recognition as the "Fifth Avenue of Montgomery" with such leading citizens in residence as businessman William Knox, Dr. W.O. Baldwin, insurance executive Robert Jones, and attorneys Jack Thorington and William Lowndes Yancey. Through the years it continued to attract those who were the city's cultural, political, social, and business leaders. (1894 *Art Works*/ Landmarks Collection.)

South Perry Street, Corner of High Street. The cottage in the right foreground was one of the first homes built on Perry Street in the late 1820s. Fences were important not just for appearances but to keep the children in and, with people still holding horses and cows in backyard barns, to prevent runaway animals from ruining lawns and gardens. (1894 *Art Works*/Landmarks Collection.)

South Perry Street, c. 1900. The trees had grown along the west side of the 500 block, and this picture postcard, designed to show off the city to its best advantage, would have encouraged people to come for a visit. (Scott/Fouts Photographic Services.)

South Perry Street, 1906. This photograph reflected the prosperity enjoyed by the people who lived on tree-lined South Perry Street. In the foreground is the home of J.M. Kennedy, a Scot who settled in Montgomery and became a manufacturer of bricks and a dealer in paints and lumber products. (Library of Congress.)

Woman's College and Cloverdale, c. 1925. This aerial photograph illustrated an area on the verge of expansion. Then called the Woman's College of Alabama, Huntingdon College was the edge of the growing village of Cloverdale, which would, in the next two years, become a

part of the city of Montgomery. The school was also to add four new buildings before the 1929 stock market crash. (Scott/Fouts Photographic Services.)

Growing Neighborhoods. In the 1920s and 1930s, residential neighborhoods continued to develop. Norman Bridge Road is on the left, with Ponce de Leon Avenue entering it in the

foreground. Fairview Avenue is in the center of the picture. (Fred Drehr Collection.)

(Left) Executive Mansion, 1906. Designed by Weatherly Carter for Adjutant General Robert Ligon in 1906, this house exemplified the renewed interest in the Neo-Classical style, a reaction to the exotic expressions of Queen Anne architecture. It has been the Executive Mansion of Alabama since the state acquired it in 1955. (John Scott, Scott Photographic Services.) **(Right) Gay-Kirkland Apartments, c. 1900, Clayton Street (Demolished).** Apartment living became popular in Montgomery around the turn of the century. One of the first dwellings of that kind was the Gay-Kirkland Flats, whose distinctive classical entranceway gave it a touch of elegance. (1907 *Art Works*/Landmarks Collection.)

Ragland House, Madison Avenue, c. 1904 (Standing). In a new architectural phase inspired by the arts and crafts movement, the Greene Brothers of California and Frank Lloyd Wright turned away from the revival styles, incorporating simpler details and more natural lines and materials. William H. Ragland, a manager for the Montgomery Traction Company, which operated the streetcars, built this home in the developing suburb of Capital Heights. (1907 *Art Works*/Landmarks Collection.)

Eight
Recreational
Corners

Parks, parades, picnics, and picture shows continue to be popular, and one or the other is around almost any corner. Montgomery has long enjoyed all, and in this chapter are samples of each.

Blues on Parade, c. 1850. One of Montgomery's first and most noted volunteer militias, the True Blues organized in 1836 in response to President Martin Van Buren's call for volunteers for the Seminole War; later, the unit served in the Mexican War. This painting, probably dating from the latter era, depicts the corps marching up Market Street in front of the Montgomery Hall. (The painting is in the collection of the Alabama Department of Archives and History.)

Alabama State Fair, 1858. *Harper's Weekly*, a leading nation-wide publication, reported on the fourth annual Alabama State Fair in its November 27, 1858 edition, illustrating it with this drawing of one of the horse shows. Commenting on the event, the writer noted that the facilities and exhibits were "commensurate with the rapidly improving interests of this young and flourishing state. . . ."(*Harper's Weekly*; Air University Library, Maxwell AFB Collection; copy print, Landmarks Collection.)

Southern Troops, 1861. A lithograph from *Harper's Weekly* of February 9, 1861, depicted a parade of Southern troops marching west on Market Street as the eyes of the nation focused on what was taking place in Montgomery, capital of the newly organized Confederate States of America. An accompanying article stated that "Montgomery is a pretty city of some nine or ten thousand inhabitants, situated on the River Alabama. It does a lively business in cotton, and its mart is one of the most important secondary marts of the South. It is expected that Montgomery will become the capital of the Southern Confederacy." (*Harper's Weekly*; Air University Library, Maxwell AFB Collection; copy print, Landmarks Collection.)

On the Way to the Station, 1898. Flower-bedecked horses, ladies, and carriages contributed to the festivities as Montgomerians celebrated the opening of the grand Union Station on May 6, 1898. These young ladies were leaving from the H.C. Davidson home on South Court Street. (Davidson/Freeborn.)

Spanish-American War, 1898. At the same time Union Station was opening with great fanfare, the United States was preparing to go to war with Spain because of several incidents, the most significant being the explosion of the battleship *Maine* in Havana Harbor. Spurred on by the efforts of the William Randolph Hearst newspapers, the United States, displaying a rising imperialistic attitude, took on that waning power, Spain. Alabamians enlisted, eager to "Remember the Maine." Here, troops march down Commerce Street to Union Station, the first military deployment through the new facilities. (ADAH.)

Street Fair Program, 1899. Autumn brought cooler weather and the annual street fairs for which people flocked to Montgomery from far and wide. Designed for pleasure and for promotion of the city, the five-day event included parades, exhibits, concerts, and feats of daring such as "Apollo, the Famous Tight Wire Walker." (Landmarks Collection.)

Street Fair, 1899. From October 23 to 28, booths lined Dexter Avenue as throngs turned out for one of several parades which marked the gala occasion. (Crane Collection.)

Street Fair Dandies, 1899. In all probability, this happy, dressed-up group of dandies and belles were on their way to participate in an 1899 street fair parade. (Crane Collection.)

Samford Funeral, 1901. While some parades brought fun and happiness, others were for sadder occasions, such as the funeral cortege of Governor W.J. Samford, which wound its way down Dexter Avenue on a rainy day in June 1901. Elected in 1900, Samford served only a few months before his death on June 11, 1901. (ADAH.)

Presidential Visit, 1905. On October 24, 1905, Theodore Roosevelt visited Montgomery during a tour through the state. His entourage was moving down South Court Street when an amateur photographer snapped his camera, recording a significant moment in his life. It wasn't everyday that the president came to town. (Sullivan Collection.)

Pageant of Businesses Parade, 1909. Promoting Montgomery, the "Pageant of the City's Businesses" parade took place on October 28, 1909, in conjunction with the Alabama Agricultural Fair. Henry Conway James, a salesman for M.P. Wilcox, wholesaler, and his driver prepared to join in the festivities. (McClurkin Collection.)

Circus Parade, c. 1911. Circus parades have delighted all ages for hundreds of years. Advertising Cook's Beer, the lead camel crossed Montgomery Street and proceeded up Lee Street in this c. 1911 photograph. (Hattemer Collection.)

Circus Parade, c. 1911. Elephants, too, advertised for local concerns, with the first promoting the Fourth National Bank and the second commending ice cream. (Hattemer Collection.)

Return of the 167th Infantry, 1919. The homecoming of Alabama's 167th Infantry Division on May 12, 1919, brought people from all over the state to the Capital City. A bevy of young ladies lined a triumphal arch on Dexter Avenue as troops marched to the Alabama State Capitol. (ADAH.)

Victory! Thousands flocked to the heart of town on May 12, 1919, to give a hero's welcome to the Alabama boys who were returning to the state as victors in a most difficult and deadly conflict. Hopes were high that this, indeed, had been the last great war. (Crook Collection.)

Brandon Inauguration, 1923.
Elected governor in 1922, W.W.
"Plain Bill" Brandon assumed office
on January 15, 1923, with an official
parade up Dexter Avenue, which the
state and city had decorated with
banners and flags for the day.
(Landmarks Collection.)

Prepared Boy Scout, 1923. A Boy
Scout stood ready to assist anyone in
need at the corner of Dexter Avenue
and South Perry Street during the
Brandon inaugural parade.
Conservatives, Brandon and his
lieutenant-governor, Charles S.
McDowell, carried out several major
programs including highway
construction, capitol renovations,
and land acquisition on Dexter
Avenue for state buildings.
(Landmarks Collection.)

Axes to Grind, 1923. Uniformed men, led by a Boy Scout, carried swords and axes as they moved up Dexter Avenue in front of Brown Printing Company at the corner of McDonough Street. Today, there is no clear explanation about why the men carried axes as Brandon assumed the governorship. (Landmarks Collection.)

Nearing the Capitol, 1923. As governor-elect Brandon's entourage neared the capitol, spectators, kept at a distance by policemen, craned for a look at the dignitaries arriving by carriage and car. (Birmingham Public Library Collection.)

Cover, *The Pageant Book*, 1926. Montgomery celebrated Alabama Homecoming Week, on May 5 and 6, 1926, with "The Spirit of the South"—two days of events including parades, speeches, concerts, and a historical pageant. *The Pageant Book* was the official program of the event. (Landmarks Collection.)

Mrs. Barrett's Float, 1926. A group of young musicians performed on the Mrs. Barrett's School of Music float during a "Spirit of the South" parade. (Landmarks Collection.)

Folsom Inauguration, 1955. "Big Jim" Folsom won a second term as governor of Alabama in the fall of 1954 and took office January 17, 1955. Photographer John Scott, standing on the roof of the Bell building, took this picture as the parade wound its way up Dexter Avenue. (Scott/Fouts Photographic Services.)

Turkey Day Parade, 1966. Longtime rivals, the football teams of Alabama State University and Tuskegee University annually meet for a Thanksgiving Day clash in Montgomery. Since 1923, a Turkey Day parade through the heart of town has been one of the event's highlights. Taken as the parade moved out of Alabama State along Jackson Street, this picture captured the excitement and anticipation of the crowd. (University Library and Resource Center, Alabama State University Collection.)

Turkey Day Parade, c. 1980. This must have been an exhilarating experience for the Boy Scouts as they marched along Dexter Avenue, which was already decorated for the Christmas season. A large crowd of spectators were on hand for the morning's activities. (University Library and Resource Center, Alabama State University Collection.)

Oak Park Trolley, c. 1910. The editor of the *Montgomery Advertiser* noted in August 1886, that "in the absence of a city park [streetcar riders] find the cemetery a favored Sunday afternoon resort." The managers of the Capital City Street Railway soon remedied the situation, for later in 1886 they purchased a tract of land on the eastern perimeter of town and began development of Highland Park, the city's first subdivision, and in conjunction with it a city park which is now Oak Park.

In the Park, c. 1902. Bama Milner, a young Montgomerian, took this photograph of a friend relaxing in Oak Park. (Range Collection.)

Oak Park Pavillion, c. 1930. The center of activity at Oak Park was the pavilion where dances took place for the soldiers stationed at Camp Sheridan during World War I. It was one of the few places in town where military men and the girls of Montgomery could meet and enjoy each others' company without criticism or gossip. In this 1930s view, the well-known Montgomery photographer Stanley Paulger found John T. Mapes and a friend enjoying the front porch. (Gorrie/Landmarks Collection.)

Pickett Springs, c. 1900. Pickett Springs, noted as the "best public resort" by the *Advertiser* on September 26, 1886, was 4 miles north of town on the former plantation home of Albert J.Pickett, who in 1851 wrote the first history of Alabama. Visitors reached the popular resort by the Western Railway until the turn of the century when the trolley company extended streetcar lines to the park. (ADAH.)

Pickett Springs Outing, c. 1900. A family group enjoyed a day at Pickett Springs, where a fanciful pavilion offered shelter for picnics and visiting, favorite pastimes of the day. (Arrington Collection.)

Company Picnic, c. 1905. The employees of the local department store, Nachman and Meertief, journeyed to Pickett Springs for a company picnic and photograph. (John and June Scott Collection.)

Mother and Daughter, c. 1905. Frances Trott and her mother were among the many who found their way to Pickett Springs. (Trott Collection.)

Ready to Celebrate, c. 1913. Nine rather serious young ladies, sporting their club banner, were ready for a celebration—party, picnic, or parade. (Pryor Collection.)

Electric Park, 1902. In 1901, as the town began its inexorable move eastward, the local utility company developed Electric Park on Three Mile Branch, out on the Line Creek Road. Utilizing electricity for the operation and lighting of several rides and pavilions, the company encouraged the population to ride the electric trolley for a day of entertainment and pleasure. Forest Hills Shopping Center is now on the site. (1907 *Art Works*/Landmarks Collection.)

Montgomery Country Club, 1904. The growing popularity of golf and tennis in the early years of the twentieth century prompted the building of country clubs. In 1904, Montgomerians built a fashionable clubhouse near the village of Cloverdale on the outskirts of the city. During World War I, dances for local belles and the soldiers stationed at Camp Sheridan spawned many romances, one of which was that between Zelda Sayre, daughter of a prominent family, and Lt. F. Scott Fitzgerald, a native of Minnesota who had already begun his writing career. Married in 1920, the two epitomized the Jazz Age for their generation. Located on Mulberry Street, the club burned to the ground in 1926. (1907 *Art Works*/Landmark Collection.)

Ladies on the Links, c. 1904. Trying their hands at the ancient game of golf, these three young ladies were on the links of the Montgomery Country Club. (Freeborn Collection.)

Golfers, c. 1904. Two gentlemen assist Fanny Lee Davidson and a friend as they prepare to tee off at the Montgomery Country Club. (Freeborn Collection.)

An Outing, c. 1910. A photographer's studio often had many different backdrops and props from which to choose, and this nattily attired group selected the very popular automobile set. (Pryor Collection.)

Lollipop Eaters, c. 1902. Photographer Bama Milner found Effie Wilson and her friends enjoying lollipops in this happy picture. (Range Collection.)

Bicycling, c. 1910. Out for a spin, this young lady was among the many who found the bicycle a means of transportation and pleasure. (Starr Collection.)

(Left) Myers Popcorn, c. 1937. From the 1920s to the 1970s, the Pop Myers operated their famous popcorn and soft drink stands which catered to young and old at two locations. Operated by brothers, both of whom were known as "Pop," one shop was on Forest Avenue at Oak Park and the other was on Fairview Avenue near Cloverdale School and its adjoining ball field. Jerome Myers was "Pop Jr." to several generations of Cloverdale School students, the firemen at the nearby station, and everybody in the neighborhood. (Windham Collection.) **(Right) Myers Popcorn, c. 1950.** Marcus B. Myers, also known as Pop, ran the Forest Avenue/Oak Park popcorn stand. Generous and compassionate, Pop frequently visited the children in a nearby hospital, taking small gifts to cheer them up. (Pugh Collection.)

The Strand. Since early in the century, picture shows have been popular sources of entertainment. Over the years, Montgomery has had many movie houses, including the Orpheum, Empire, Charles, Rogers, Tivoli, Highland, Clover, Carver, Pekin, Paramount, and Strand. Located on the west side of Court Square, the Strand, not quite as decorative as the Paramount, was a popular spot. (Collier/Landmarks Collection.)

The Paramount, on Montgomery Street. Although the Strand has been demolished, the Paramount, restored and re-christened the Davis Theater, provides the setting for many musical and dramatic events, including the Montgomery Symphony, the Alabama Dance Theater, and the Montgomery Civic Ballet performances. (Collier/Landmarks Collection.)

Nine
Rounding Corners

The cornerstones of a city are often transitory; consequently, it is important for each generation to explore the records of the past—photographs, documents, archaeological remains, and reminiscences—to study and to preserve them for the future. Photographs tell many stories about a community. Some illustrate the relationships of the people, some depict the changing environment and a few snapshots vividly describe hazards sometimes involved in rounding corners too sharply or too carelessly. This chapter has no overall theme except the concept that photographs can educate, explain, and entertain.

Flivver Flop, c. 1914. Was the driver of this flivver speeding down South Hull Street, jumping the curb as he crossed Felder Avenue? Trinity Presbyterian Church is in the background. (ADAH.)

Collision! This was a real calamity, with two firetrucks put out of commission after a collision at the intersection of Jefferson and North Hull Streets on March 11, 1943. Rushing to a fire, an

engine and a hook-and-ladder truck ran into each other, creating quite a mess at the corner and great consternation for the firemen involved. (Scott/Fouts Photographic Services.)

Road Scraper #1, c. 1920. Even in urban Montgomery there were unpaved roads which required the services of a road scraper. In this photograph, the tractor driver and the man on the scraper seemed to have everything in order. (ADAH.)

Road Scraper #2, c. 1920. Obviously, something went awry, for the scraper overturned, creating a problem for the workmen. However, the wreck provided entertainment for the child in the window. (ADAH.)

Cotton on the Corner, 1906. Cotton was around almost any corner of downtown Montgomery during the picking season. This photograph was taken at the intersection of Tallapoosa and Columbus Streets. (Maurer Collection.)

Corner Grocery, 1890s. A most essential part of any neighborhood was the corner grocery where all segments of the population met on more or less equal terms on a daily basis. This store fronted both South Hull and Julia Streets. (1894 *Art Works*/Landmarks Collection.)

For the Fun of It, c. 1914. Frank Walker Cargill and this goat, Bill, enjoyed a summertime trip to Oak Park, just across the street from Frank's home on Stevenson Street. (Cargill/McDuffee Collection.)

Again, For the Fun of It, c. 1933. The Hobbie family owned Hobbie Motor Car Company, which in the 1930s was on Madison Avenue. However, they did not confine their interests to ground transportation, for in 1933 members of the family built an airplane, proudly displayed here in front of their company. (Hobbie/Landmarks Collection.)